T0199020

Find Joy, Give Grace!!

BY JESSICA MITCHUM

WestBow Press books may be ordered through booksellers or by contacting:

WestBow Press
A Division of Thomas Nelson & Zondervan
1663 Liberty Drive
Bloomington, IN 47403
www.westbowpress.com
844.714.3454

Because of the dynamic nature of the Internet, any web addresses or links contained in this book may have changed since publication and may no longer be valid. The views expressed in this work are solely those of the author and do not necessarily reflect the views of the publisher, and the publisher hereby disclaims any responsibility for them.

Image Credit: Jessica, Michelle, and Hannah Mitchum

Scripture quotations marked (TLB) are taken from The Living Bible copyright © 1971. Used by permission of Tyndale House Publishers, a Division of Tyndale House Ministries, Carol Stream, Illinois 60188. All rights reserved.

Scripture marked (ERV) taken from the Holy Bible: Easy-to-Read Version (ERV), International Edition © 2013, 2016 by Bible League International and used by permission.

Scripture quotations marked (NIV) are taken from the Holy Bible, New International Version®, NIV®. Copyright © 1973, 1978, 1984, 2011 by Biblica, Inc.® Used by permission of Zondervan. All rights reserved worldwide. www.zondervan.com The "NIV" and "New International Version" are trademarks registered in the United States Patent and Trademark Office by Biblica, Inc.®

Scripture quotations marked (ESV) are from the ESV® Bible (The Holy Bible, English Standard Version®), copyright © 2001 by Crossway, a publishing ministry of Good News Publishers. Used by permission. All rights reserved.

ISBN: 978-1-6642-0208-5 (sc)
ISBN: 978-1-6642-0209-2 (e)

Library of Congress Control Number: 2020915289

Print information available on the last page.

WestBow Press rev. date: 09/04/2020

WESTBOW
P R E S S®
A DIVISION OF THOMAS NELSON
& ZONDERVAN

Table of Contents

Thank you, Hannah, for your enthusiastic joy!

Michelle, thanks for your contagious desire to give God your best!

I've Found Joy!

Where do I go to look for joy?

Do I find it in a new toy?

Things make me
happy awhile...

It is so fun to
play and smile!

Joy is something
even better!

I can find joy
in whatever!

3

God made the whole world and me too!

4

Christ lives! That's what true joy's about!

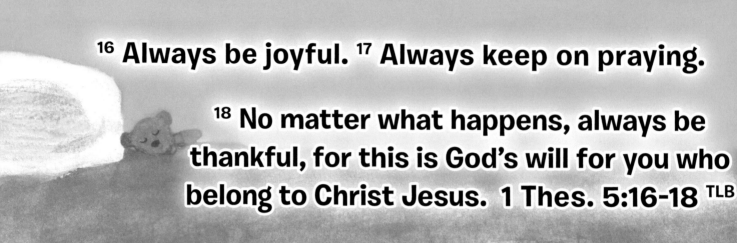

16 Always be joyful. **17** Always keep on praying.

18 No matter what happens, always be thankful, for this is God's will for you who belong to Christ Jesus. 1 Thes. 5:16-18 ᵀᴸᴮ

True Love?

Love is patient.

It waits for as long as it takes...

Like waiting for cookies to bake.

Love is kind,

So we should care
for each other,

Like when you comfort
your brother.

Love's not jealous,

Like how you decided to share.

When you do, it shows friends you care.

Love forgives,

Doesn't matter what kind of ouch.

We should love and not be a grouch.

Love never ends.

True love goes on
and on and on!

God's love we can
always lean upon!

⁴ Love is patient and kind. Love is not jealous, it does not brag, and it is not proud. ⁵ Love is not rude, it is not selfish, and it cannot be made angry easily. Love does not remember wrongs done against it. ⁸ᵃ Love will never end. 1 Cor. 13:4-5, 8a ᴱᴿⱽ

John 13:14

!יהוה

One Hope

15

Look at the news and we see hate.
Jesus is our hope from sin's fate.

Don't put your hope in me or you.

Don't experts mostly guess off clues?

When's my job done?

God sees beauty in all He made.
His love for all will never fade.

Jesus is patient and humble.
Let all race divisions crumble!

Should money or race divide? Nope!
There's one saving faith, He's our hope!

19

May all our voices
praise in verse,

The God who made
the universe!

² **Be completely humble and gentle; be patient, bearing with one another in love. ⁴ There is one body and one Spirit, just as you were called to one hope when you were called; ⁵ one Lord, one faith, one baptism; ⁶ one God and Father of all... Eph. 4:2, 4-6a** ᴺᴵⱽ

Given Grace!

8 For by grace you have been saved through faith. And this is not your own doing; it is the gift of God, 9 not a result of works, so that no one may boast. Ephesians 2:8-9 ESV

What is your favorite gift ever?
Something that you'll love forever?

Great gifts are meant to show you love.

God sent His son down from above.

Jesus chose to die for our sins,

Our guilt is gone, new life begins!

Our best falls so short on our own.

Thank you Lord for the grace you've shown!

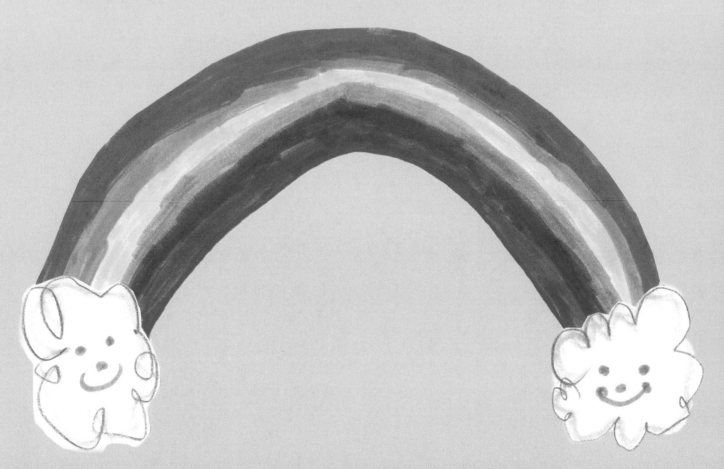

Trust in Jesus's love to see,

What His good plans
for you will be!

Find Joy, Give Grace!!

Do you need help finding joy or giving grace? Everyone does! Growing is slow... But if you decide to follow Jesus, then the Holy Spirit is always ready to help you find joy in Jesus and grow in grace!

Do you know Jesus?

Because, if you confess with your mouth that Jesus is Lord and believe in your heart that God raised him from the dead, you will be saved. Rom. 10:9 ESV

APPENDIX: WHAT'S HEAVEN LIKE?

People from every nation will be there! ❯ ... there before me was a great multitude that no one could count, from every nation, tribe, people and language, standing before the throne and before the Lamb. They were wearing white robes and were holding palm branches in their hands. (Rev. 7:9b NIV)

Jesus' followers get to be with Him! ❯ After I go and prepare a place for you, I will come back. Then I will take you with me, so that you can be where I am. (John 14:3 ERV)

A real and beautiful place! ❯ 19 The foundations of the city walls were decorated with every kind of precious stone... 21 The twelve gates were twelve pearls, each gate made of a single pearl. The great street of the city was of gold, as pure as transparent glass. (Rev. 21:19a, 21 NIV)

No more death! ❯ He will wipe away every tear from their eyes. There will be no more death, sadness, crying, or pain. All the old ways are gone. (Rev. 21:4 ERV)

Perfect peace! ❯ The wolf and the lamb will feed together, and the lion will eat straw like the ox... (Isa. 65:25a NIV)

Better than you can imagine! ❯ ... "No eye has seen, no ear has heard, and no mind has imagined the things that God has prepared for those who love him." (1 Cor. 2:9b ISV)

On Page 17 what did the funny letters above the gate mean? That's "Judah," in Hebrew. See Rev. 21:12 for details.

Printed in the United States
By Bookmasters